D1028064

SIMCOE STREET SCHOOL
Niagara Falls, Ont.

SIMCOE STREET SCHOOL
Niagara Falls, Ont.

SHIPPED NOV 29 2010

Crabapples

Space

Bobbie Kalman & Niki Walker

Crabtree Publishing Company

Crabapples

created by Bobbie Kalman

For Leeland, my favorite space case
xo

Editor-in-Chief
Bobbie Kalman

Writing team
Bobbie Kalman
Niki Walker

Managing editor
Lynda Hale

Editors
Greg Nickles
Petrina Gentile

Computer design
Lucy DeFazio
Lynda Hale

Color separations and film
Dot 'n Line Image Inc.

Special thanks to
NASA; Jean-Guy Monette and the National Museum of Science and Technology; and Astronaut Robert L. Crippen shown on page 28

Photographs and digital enhancements
Francois Gohier/Photo Researchers, Inc.: page 22 (bottom)
NASA: title page, pages 25, 28, 30 (both)
NASA/Science Source/Photo Researchers, Inc: page 18
Jerry Schad/Photo Researchers, Inc.: page 23
Tom Stack & Associates: Bill and Sally Fletcher: pages 4-5; Inga Spence: page 27; ESA/TSADO: page 13 (top); JPL/TSADO: pages 11, 12 (both), 22 (top); NASA/ESA: page 19; NASA/JPL: cover, page 17; NASA/JPL/TSADO: pages 9, 15, 16 (inset), 20 (bottom); NASA: pages 14 (bottom), 26; NASA/TSADO: pages 6-7; NOAA/TSADO: page 10; Rockwell/TSADO: page 21; TSADO: pages 13 (bottom), 16, 20 (top); USGS/NASA/TSADO: page 14 (top)

Printer
Worzalla Publishing Company

Crabtree Publishing Company

PMB 16A
350 Fifth Ave.,
Suite 3308
N.Y., N.Y. 10118

612 Welland Ave.,
St. Catharines,
Ontario, Canada
L2M 5V6

73 Lime Walk
Headington
Oxford OX3 7AD
United Kingdom

Copyright © **1997 CRABTREE PUBLISHING COMPANY**.
All rights reserved. No part of this publication may be reproduced, stored in a retrieval system or be transmitted in any form or by any means, electronic, mechanical, photocopying, recording, or otherwise, without the prior written permission of Crabtree Publishing Company.

Cataloging in Publication Data
Kalman, Bobbie
  Space
(Crabapples)
Includes index.
ISBN 0-86505-638-2 (library bound) ISBN 0-86505-738-9 (pbk.)
This book introduces the universe, solar system, stars, planets, asteroids, satellites, and space travel.

1. Astronomy - Juvenile literature. 2. Planets - Juvenile literature. 3. Astronautics - Juvenile literature. 4. Outer space - Exploration - Juvenile literature. 5. Space biology - Juvenile literature. I. Walker, Niki. II.Title. III. Series: Kalman, Bobbie. Crabapples.
QB46.K353 1997   j520   LC 97-3640
                                                 CIP

What is in this book?

What is out there?

Do you ever wonder what lies beyond our sky? About 75 miles (120 km) above your head, space begins. Everything out there, including stars, planets, moons, rocks, dust, and gas, is part of space, or the **universe**.

The universe is much larger than any person can imagine. Earth seems big to us, but it is only one of nine planets orbiting our Sun. The Sun is just one of the billions of stars in our **Galaxy**, the **Milky Way**. There are billions of other galaxies in the universe!

Most scientists believe that the universe began about 15 billion years ago, with a huge explosion called the **Big Bang**. The force of the Big Bang was so great that all the galaxies in the universe are still being pushed outward because of it. This movement of the galaxies means that the universe is getting larger every second. Scientists are not certain exactly how big the universe is, but some believe it does not have an end. It may stretch on forever!

Stars

On a clear night, away from the lights of cities and towns, you can see a few thousand stars without using a telescope. All the stars are in our own Galaxy. Stars are balls of burning gases. They form inside clouds of dust and gas called **nebulae**.

Small stars are about the size of a large city. Large stars are 100 times bigger than our Sun. Stars appear white when we look at them without a telescope, but they are many different colors. The hottest stars are bluish white, the coolest are red, and those between are yellow or orange.

In our night sky, stars often form patterns that look like animals, people, or objects. These patterns are **constellations**. There are 88 different constellations. You can find some of them with a **star chart**, which is a map of the night sky. People who live north of the equator see different constellations than those who live south of the equator. Different constellations appear in the summer than in the winter.

The solar system

Scientists believe that the solar system formed about 4.5 billion years ago. It includes the Sun, the nine planets that orbit it, their moons, and all the dust, ice, and rocks among them.

The four planets closest to the Sun are the **inner planets**. The next four are the **outer planets**. They are larger than the inner planets. They are also much colder because they are farther from the Sun. Outer planets are made up mostly of gases, but the inner ones are rocky.

The ninth planet, Pluto, is not part of either group. It is far from the Sun, but scientists believe it is solid, like the inner planets. There also may be a tenth, small planet just beyond Pluto. It is called Planet X.

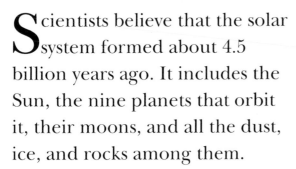

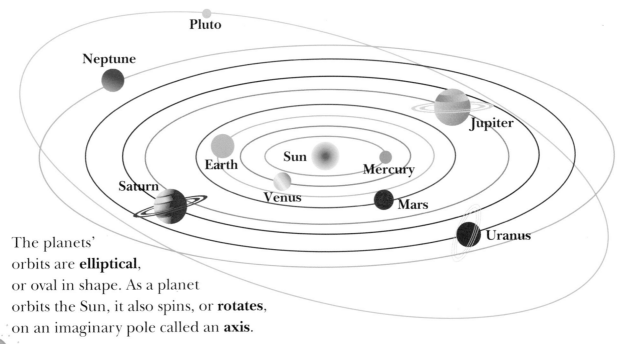

The planets' orbits are **elliptical**, or oval in shape. As a planet orbits the Sun, it also spins, or **rotates**, on an imaginary pole called an **axis**.

These are all the planets in the solar system except Pluto. In space, they are not as close to one another as they appear here.

The Sun

The Sun is a star. Energy is made in its center, which is the hottest part. The energy moves out from the center and into the solar system. The Sun is so far away that this energy, called **solar energy**, takes over eight minutes to travel to Earth! The energy reaches us as heat and light. Without it, there would be no life on our planet. Someday, the Sun will burn out, or die. Scientists believe, however, that its death is at least 5 billion years away.

Mercury

Mercury is the second-smallest planet. It is the only known planet on which a day is longer than a year. A year is the time it takes a planet to orbit the Sun. A year on Mercury lasts only 59 days. A day is measured from sunrise to sunrise. On Mercury, the time between one sunrise and the next is 180 Earth days!

Venus

Venus is almost the same size as Earth. It is also the nearest planet to ours. Scientists once believed that the surface of Venus was similar to that of Earth, but now they know it is very different. Venus has an atmosphere that traps the Sun's heat. During the day, it can be 900°F (480°C) on Venus! This temperature is hot enough to melt some kinds of metal in seconds.

Earth

Earth is the only planet known to have liquid water. More than 70% of its surface is covered with water. Earth is nicknamed the "blue planet" because, from space, all its water makes the planet appear blue. On Earth, the time between one sunrise and the next is almost 24 hours. It takes Earth about 365 days to orbit the Sun.

Mars

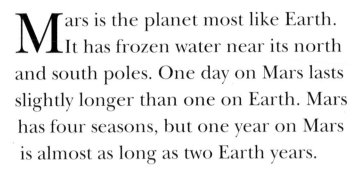

Mars is the planet most like Earth. It has frozen water near its north and south poles. One day on Mars lasts slightly longer than one on Earth. Mars has four seasons, but one year on Mars is almost as long as two Earth years.

In a rock from Mars, scientists found remains of life. They may have been left by creatures that were very tiny, or **microscopic**. They probably lived on Mars more than 3 billion years ago.

Jupiter

Jupiter is the largest planet. It is a thousand times bigger than Earth! It has 16 moons, and four of them are as large as planets. The big red spot on Jupiter's surface is a huge storm that has been raging for over 300 years! This storm is large enough to surround three planets the size of Earth.

Like the other outer planets, Jupiter is not solid. It is made up mainly of gases, so it does not have a hard surface that you could stand on. Jupiter and the other outer planets have rings around them. Jupiter's rings, however, are too thin to be seen from Earth.

Saturn

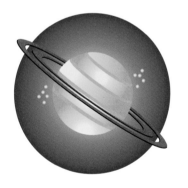

Saturn is the second-largest planet in the solar system. It has 18 moons. Saturn is the only planet with rings that can be seen from Earth. The rings are not solid. They are made up of millions of small pieces of rock, dust, and ice that orbit the planet.

Uranus

Uranus was the first planet discovered with a telescope, in 1781. Uranus is four times larger than Earth, and has 15 moons and 11 rings.

Uranus spins differently than the other planets in the solar system. They spin upright, like tops, but Uranus rotates on its side, like a rolling ball.

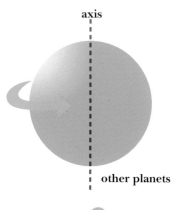

axis

other planets

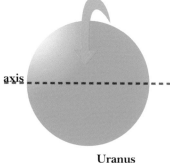

axis

Uranus

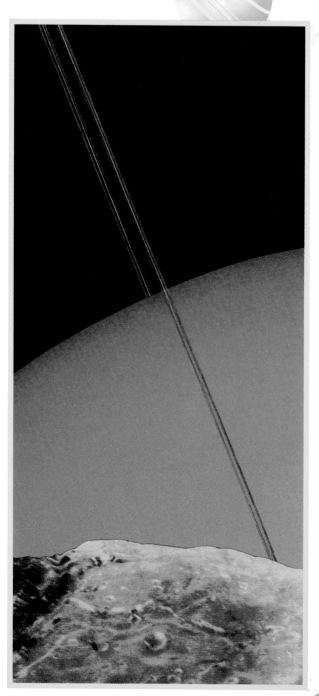

Neptune

Neptune is so far from Earth that it is difficult to see, even with a powerful telescope. It was found in 1846. Neptune has eight known moons and four rings. It has small white clouds that look similar to those of Earth. Neptune, like Jupiter and Saturn, has storms that last for years—even centuries! Neptune's winds may be the fastest in the solar system.

Pluto

Pluto is the smallest planet. Some outer planets have moons that are as large as Pluto! Pluto is the farthest planet from the Sun. It takes Pluto about 249 Earth years to orbit the Sun once! Pluto is so far away from Earth that it was not found until 1930. Even with the strongest telescope, it is still difficult to see Pluto.

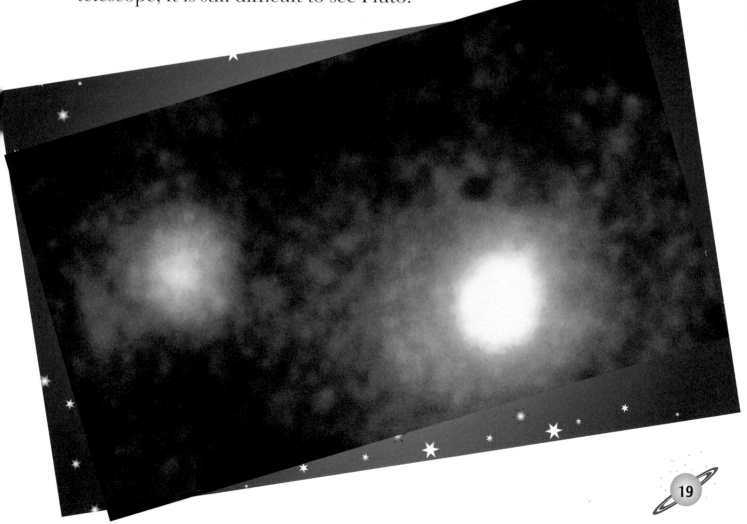

The Moon and other satellites

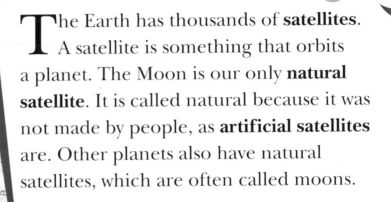

The Earth has thousands of **satellites**. A satellite is something that orbits a planet. The Moon is our only **natural satellite**. It is called natural because it was not made by people, as **artificial satellites** are. Other planets also have natural satellites, which are often called moons.

Our Moon is the only object in the solar system on which astronauts have landed. The first person to step onto it was an American astronaut named Neil Armstrong, in 1969. Any footprints left on the Moon's dusty surface could stay there for billions of years. There is no wind or rain to erase them. There is no atmosphere, so astronauts must wear special suits that give them oxygen to breathe. The suits also protect astronauts from the very hot and cold temperatures on the moon. People weigh much less on the Moon because its **gravity** is much weaker than the Earth's.

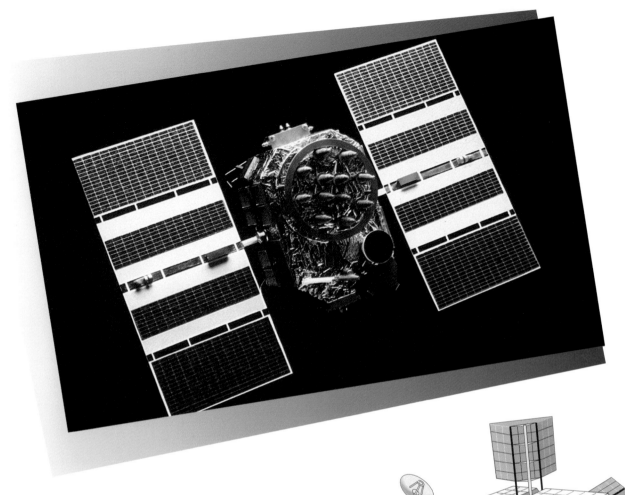

People launch different types of artificial satellites to perform different jobs. Weather satellites allow scientists to watch cloud movement, which helps them predict weather. Some communications satellites allow people to make overseas telephone calls and trade information between computers. Others broadcast pictures to television sets around the world in seconds. Satellites are also used to watch the movement of oil spills, forest fires, and other environmental disasters.

Asteroids, meteors, and comets

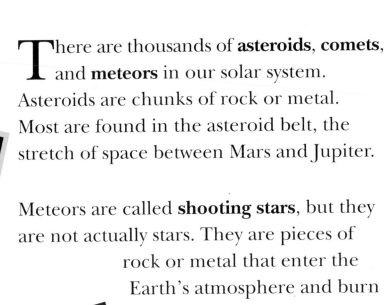

There are thousands of **asteroids**, **comets**, and **meteors** in our solar system. Asteroids are chunks of rock or metal. Most are found in the asteroid belt, the stretch of space between Mars and Jupiter.

Meteors are called **shooting stars**, but they are not actually stars. They are pieces of rock or metal that enter the Earth's atmosphere and burn as they fall through it. Most meteors are smaller than pebbles. They burn up in less than one second.

Sometimes a meteor does not burn up completely, however. A meteor that reaches the ground is called a **meteorite**. The crater on the left was made by a meteorite. About 500 meteorites hit the ground each year, but there is only one record of a person being hit by one.

Comets orbit the Sun. They have two parts—a **head** and **tail**. Scientists believe that the head of a comet is a hard ball of ice and dust. When it comes close to the Sun, the ball begins to melt. Wind from the Sun blows the dust and melted ice into a bright tail behind the head. Most comets last a few weeks, until they travel away from the heat of the Sun and their head freezes again.

Exploring space

Many of the things we know about our solar system were discovered using **space probes**. Space probes are machines that are sent up to land on or fly past other planets and send pictures back to Earth. Space probes give us information about the surfaces of planets. Some can land on planets that are too hot or poisonous for people.

People in space

The first person sent into space was a Russian **cosmonaut** named Yuri Gagarin, in 1961. His trip lasted just under two hours. Since then, many other astronauts and spacecraft have been launched. Their trips lasted much longer than Gagarin's.

Space shuttles

Many types of spacecraft have been invented. The **space shuttle** is one of the newest. Other spacecraft can be launched only once, but a space shuttle can be sent into space several times. It spends about two weeks orbiting Earth. While in orbit, astronauts do experiments and repair satellites.

space shuttle with booster rockets

space shuttle

Space stations

A **space station** is a spacecraft that orbits Earth. It can stay in space for years at a time. On a space station, astronauts conduct experiments to make new and better medicines. They observe how plants grow without gravity. They study what happens to people's bodies after being in space for a long time. All this information may help people live in space someday.

Mir space station

Partners in space

The United States, Russia, Canada, and other countries are working together to build the International Space Station (ISS). **Modules**, such as laboratories, will be launched from Earth and assembled in space. To practice building the ISS, astronauts are working with cosmonauts on the Russian space station *Mir*, which has been in orbit since 1986.

Is anyone there?

Scientists use **radio telescopes** to search space for radio waves from alien beings that may be living outside our solar system. In 1974, a message was sent in the direction of a star that is near our solar system. We cannot expect a quick reply, however. The star is so far that it will take 25,000 years for the message to reach any planets around it!

What is it like in space?

Have you ever wondered what it is like to be in space? Everything, including people, becomes weightless because there is no gravity.

Hard on the body

It takes time to get used to weightlessness. Some astronauts feel dizzy and nauseous from space sickness. Bones and muscles, including the heart, become weaker. To stay healthy, astronauts must exercise several hours a day.

Life without gravity

Things we do easily on Earth, such as eating, sleeping, and even flushing a toilet become tricky without gravity! Water, food, or sleeping astronauts floating inside a spacecraft could damage the controls. Special foods, toilets, and sleeping gear must be used.

Making and eating food

Food that is taken into space is dried, or **dehydrated**. Dehydrated food does not spoil and takes up little room. Water is added before eating. Meal trays are fastened to the astronauts' legs. Dishes are attached to them by Velcro®, and magnets hold the forks and knives.

Space toilets

Space toilets use strong jets of air to blow wastes into a bag below the toilet. The wastes are dried and stored. To stay seated, astronauts slide their feet under bars at the bottom of the toilet and fasten straps across their legs.

Sleeping without drifting off

Astronauts sleep in sleeping bags. They are strapped in so they do not float around while they sleep. Their pillow is stuck to the sleeping bag with Velcro®.

Air and air pressure

Outside a space shuttle, there is no air to breathe and no air pressure. Without air pressure, a person's blood would boil. Temperatures in space range from -250°F (-157°C) to 250°F (121°C). To work outside, or **space walk**, an astronaut must wear a space suit called an EMU. It has air pressure, oxygen, and temperature controls.

Staying attached

Astronauts fasten themselves to the space shuttle to keep from drifting into space. To work on things away from the shuttle, such as damaged satellites, astronauts use an MMU. An MMU attaches to a space suit. It looks like an armchair with controls on each arm that allow the astronaut to fly in different directions.

Words to know

atmosphere The layer of gases around some planets and moons

axis An imaginary line or pole that passes through a planet, on which the planet spins

cosmonaut A Russian astronaut

galaxy A huge grouping of stars and the gas and dust among them

gravity The force that pulls one object toward another, as people are pulled toward the Earth's center

inner planet Any of the four small, rocky planets closest to the Sun

module A section of a spacecraft that has a certain function, such as a lab

moon An object that naturally orbits a planet

orbit To travel around another object, as planets orbit the Sun and space shuttles orbit the Earth

outer planet Any of our solar system's large, gassy planets—Jupiter, Saturn, Uranus, and Neptune

planet A large object that orbits a star and does not make its own light

radio telescope An instrument that detects radio waves from space

telescope A piece of equipment that allows a person to see distant objects

Index

What is in the picture?

Here is more information about the photographs in this book.

page:		page:	
cover	The Galileo probe flies past Jupiter and one of its moons, Io.	17	Uranus has 11 rings, but they cannot be seen from Earth.
title page:	An astronaut space walks to repair a satellite.	18	It takes Neptune 165 Earth years to orbit the Sun once.
4-5	Our neighboring galaxy is called the Andromeda Galaxy.	19	Pluto may actually be a large asteroid. It is the larger object in the photo. Its moon, Charon, is the smaller one next to it.
6-7	Stars become cooler and change color as they grow older.		
9	This is not a real photograph of our solar system. It has been created on a computer.	20 (top)	This astronaut was part of one of the Apollo missions to the Moon.
10	The Sun is large enough to hold one million Earths!	20 (bottom)	This photo shows the far side of the Moon, which can never be seen from Earth.
11	On Mercury, you would weigh only 1/3 of your weight on Earth.	21	A Global Positioning Satellite (GPS) helps navigate ships and planes.
12 (top)	Venus is often the second-brightest object in our night sky.	22 (top)	Asteroids are also known as **minor planets**.
12 (bottom)	Venus has volcanoes that may be active.	22 (bottom)	This crater, made by a huge meteorite, is in Arizona.
13 (top)	Earth is 7,926 miles (12 756 km) wide.	23	Comets have tails that are millions of miles long.
13 (bottom)	Earth as seen from the Moon's surface	25	The space shuttle Challenger
14 (top)	Mars is often called the "red planet."	26	Up to six people can live and work on the space station *Mir*.
14 (bottom)	This photo of Mars's surface was taken by the Viking 2 probe.	27	This huge radio telescope is found in California.
15	Some parts of Jupiter rotate faster than others.	28	An astronaut floats weightless aboard a space shuttle.
16 (top)	Saturn's rings are hundreds of thousands of miles across.	30	A space suit protects an astronaut from bits of rock and metal that float around in space.
16 (bottom)	Saturn's rings were discovered by Galileo Galilei, in 1610.	30 (inset)	This astronaut is using an MMU.

32

4 5 6 7 8 9 0 Printed in USA 6 5 4 3 2 1 0